Giovanni Battista Polacco, George Porter

An exhortation to frequent communion

Giovanni Battista Polacco, George Porter

An exhortation to frequent communion

ISBN/EAN: 9783742835871

Manufactured in Europe, USA, Canada, Australia, Japa

Cover: Foto ©Lupo / pixelio.de

Manufactured and distributed by brebook publishing software
(www.brebook.com)

Giovanni Battista Polacco, George Porter

An exhortation to frequent communion

AN EXHORTATION
TO FREQUENT COMMUNION.

BY

FATHER JOHN BAPTIST POLACCO,

PRIEST OF THE ORATORY OF PADUA.

𝔗𝔯𝔞𝔫𝔰𝔩𝔞𝔱𝔢𝔡 𝔣𝔯𝔬𝔪 𝔱𝔥𝔢 𝔍𝔱𝔞𝔩𝔦𝔞𝔫

BY THE

REV. GEORGE PORTER, S.J.

LONDON:
BURNS AND OATES.
——
1879.

CONTENTS.

———

AN EXHORTATION OF WONDERFUL CONSOLATION
TO ALL SOULS DEVOTED TO THE SACRAMENT
OF THE BLESSED EUCHARIST, WHO OFTEN
RECEIVE IT, FOR THE PURE GLORY OF GOD,
FOR THE SAKE OF THEIR OWN SALVATION,
AND FOR THE BENEFIT OF ALL THE FAITH-
FUL, LIVING AND DEAD.

BELOVED SOULS, devoted to the Sacrament of
the Altar, let talkers talk, but do you frequently
approach the Eucharistic Banquet, where all
good things are spread for you. For if, as
St. Francis of Sales tells us, the hares on certain
mountains become white during the winter,
because they see snow on all sides and live
only on snow, you, by frequently feeding your
souls on that which is Beauty, Purity, and Goodness itself, must become beautiful, pure, good
and holy.

Jesus Christ instituted the august Sacrament
of the Eucharist, wherein His Body and His
Blood are really and truly contained, " in order
that those who eat thereof may live for ever."

B

Wherefore, as you frequently partake of this Sacrament, you place the health and life of your soul in such security that it becomes, in a manner, impossible that you should be poisoned by any wicked affection.   In fact, no one can feed on this Bread of Life, and at the same time cherish in his heart any deadly affection.   As men whilst in the earthly Paradise could not die the death of the body because of the Tree of Life which God had planted there, so you cannot die spiritually because of the Sacrament of Life, of which you partake.

If the most perishable fruits, when preserved, are easily kept from destruction, surely your hearts, though frail and weak, may be preserved from the corruption of sin by the Blessed Flesh of the Son of God !

Those Christians who shall be condemned to Hell, will be struck dumb when their just Judge shall show them the guilt of their spiritual death, as they might so easily have kept the life and health of their souls by partaking of His Body, which He had bequeathed to them to be their food.   Ye accursed, He will say, how came you to die, having at hand the Fruit and Food of Life ?

§ I.

WHY DO YOU COMMUNICATE SO FREQUENTLY?

O souls, enamoured of Christ in the Blessed Sacrament, if worldly persons should ever ask you why you communicate so frequently, tell them you do so in order to learn to love God, to purify your soul from every imperfection, to be released from your miseries, to find comfort in your afflictions, to regain your strength when you are exhausted, to recover your health when you are sick.

Tell them two distinct classes of persons are bound to communicate frequently. The perfect, in order that they may remain perfect and advance in perfection; and the imperfect, in order that they may acquire perfection. The strong, lest otherwise they become stricken with weakness; the weak, that they may become strong. The sick, that they may be healed; the robust, that they may not sicken. And inasmuch as you confess yourselves imperfect, weak, and sickly, tell them you stand in need of frequent Communion, that you may acquire perfection, that you may gain strength, that you may take medicine for your ailments.

Tell them that not only are those bound to communicate frequently who are free from much worldly business, inasmuch as they enjoy the opportunity, but those also who are burdened with affairs, inasmuch as they stand in need of frequent Communion. When a man undergoes severe labour and feels exhaustion, he must take nourishment frequently.

Tell them it is folly to wrap a rich jewel in a napkin ; tell them when plants are not watered, the flowers by degrees lose their brilliancy, they droop, and cease to exhale their fragrance.

Tell them that you communicate frequently, because frequent Communion redounds to the greater glory of the Most Blessed Trinity, which is really present in the Eucharist by *concomitance ;* because it redounds to the increase of the accidental glory of Jesus Christ, of Holy Mary, and of all the saints ; and, lastly, because it gives relief to the souls of Purgatory.

Tell them that you communicate frequently because you feel the want of light, of aid, of strength, of consolation, in order to resist temptations, to break the energy of your passions, to rouse yourself to greater devotion, to exercise acts of faith, hope, and charity, to obtain spiritual joy, to participate in the merits of Jesus Christ, and to secure a certain pledge of everlasting glory.

Tell them you communicate frequently in obedience to the directions of the Councils and the Fathers, and because from the time of the institution of the Blessed Eucharist to the present day, frequent Communion was never forbidden by the Apostles, by the Popes, the Councils, or the Fathers ; but on the contrary, daily Communion was commended and recommended by them.

Tell them, finally, that you communicate frequently because the Fathers of the Church, in their explanation of the fourth petition of the Lord's Prayer, taught by Jesus Christ, consider the Eucharist to be that Bread which St. Matthew calls supersubstantial, and St. Luke our daily bread.

§ II.

THE SAINTS IN FAVOUR OF FREQUENT COMMUNION.

St. Augustine writes, " Eat every day, that every day you may gain strength.* O Christian soul, if thou wish to preserve thy beauty, never quit the table of thy Heavenly Spouse ; if thou wouldst live for ever, every day eat His Flesh.† You sin every day (by sins that are venial, and not habitual), communicate daily ; live so that you may communicate every day.‡

St. Ambrose.—If He is our daily bread, why dost thou wish to communicate only at the beginning of the year ? Live in such a manner that you may communicate every day. He who is not fit to communicate every day, will not be worthy at the end of a year.§

St. John Chrysostom.—It is not rashness to approach the altar frequently, but it is rashness to receive unworthily, even once.‖ Each day let us go in quest of this Heavenly Bread. Feed us, O Lord, with this daily bread ; daily give us this Heavenly Bread.¶

---

* Serm. 20, In verba Dni.   † Serm. 4, In fer.
‡ Serm. 23, In verba Dni.   § Lib. 5, De Sac. c. 15.
‖ Hom. 5, In Ep. 1 ad Tim.   ¶ Hom. 9, In Matt.

St. Basil.—Daily Communion is praiseworthy and useful.*

St. Cyril.—Let us ask that this Heavenly Bread be given to us every day.†

St. Paschasius.—This Bread is ours, because it is necessary to us: hence we pray that the Bread which has been given to us, may be really given to us every day.‡

St. Cyprian.—We ask for this Bread every day, in order that we may not be separated from Christ by any sin.§

St. Thomas draws a distinction as follows. As regards the Sacrament Itself, it is useful to communicate daily in order to participate in Its fruits; as regards the person who receives, it is also useful to communicate daily, if he be well prepared.

And in his answer to the first objection he says, "Since man every day stands in need of the life-giving grace of Jesus Christ, he may laudably communicate every day." ‖

This Sacrament is the food of the soul; and as the food of the body is eaten daily, so may this Sacrament be laudably received every day.

* Ep. 298, aa Cæs. Pat.   † Serm. 6, In verba Dni.
‡ In verba, "Panem nostrum," &c.   § In Orat Dom.
‖ 3, q. 80, a 10.

Hence our Lord teaches to pray, Give us this day our daily bread.

St. Jerome declares that daily Communion was in accordance with the tradition of the Church, and that in Rome the faithful were accustomed to communicate every day.*

St. Anacletus, Pope.—After the consecration let all communicate, unless they wish to be put out of the church ; for this is commanded by the Apostles, and the Holy Roman Church retains this practice.†

St. Clement.—Any of the faithful who enter the church to hear the Word of God, and abstain from Holy Communion, should be put forth as disturbers of the order of the church.

Father Thomas Bosius informs us that the *Council of Antioch*, held about the time of the Council of Nice, excommunicated all who assisted at Mass without going to Holy Communion.‡

The Council of Trent.—The Sacred Council would wish all the faithful who assist at Mass, to communicate every day, not only spiritually, but also sacramentally.§

* Ep. 28 and 50.   † Cap. "Si quis."
‡ Lib. 13, c. 5, tom. 1.   § Sess. 22, cap. 6.

The Catechism of St. Pius V.—It will be the duty of the parish priest frequently to remind the faithful that as they daily require corporal food to support life, so they should daily receive this Blessed Sacrament for the spiritual nourishment of their souls.

St. Charles Borromeo inculcates the same teaching in the Third Council of Milan.

Lastly, the *Congregation of Cardinals* (vol. iv. of the Decisions of the Sacred Rota) pronounced against a bishop who had decided that lay persons should only communicate on Sundays, Wednesdays, and Fridays, on the ground that such a decree was in opposition to the Council of Trent and the ancient practice of the Church.

This decision was given in January, 1787. In ancient times, after the consecration, all who were present communicated, and therefore it is lawful to receive the Blessed Eucharist every day. The faithful should be reminded that as they sin daily, so they should make daily use of the remedy.

§ III.

INSTANCES OF PERSONS WHO RECEIVED THE HOLY COMMUNION DAILY.

The Holy Apostles, the Martyrs, and the early Christians communicated every day.

St. Paulinus gave his monks Holy Communion every day.

St. Apollonius exhorted his flock to daily Communion.

The Abbot Apollo, the director of five hundred monks, ordered that no one should partake of his bodily food, unless he had first communicated.

St. Simon Stylites communicated every day. So did St. Bonaventure, St. Teresa, the Blessed Salvatore dell' Orta, St. Catharine of Siena, St. Charles, St. Philip Neri, St. Felix the Capuchin, St. Francis Borgia, and others. Father John Baptist of Foligno, a secular, communicated every day during sixty years. Many others followed the same practice, knowing that the soul is filled with grace in Holy Communion, that she receives a pledge of eternal glory, and that she commemorates the Passion of Jesus Christ, that she is vivified invigorated, enlightened, sustained, and united to Jesus Christ; that she advances in virtue, in peace, and in joy; that she resists the temptations of the devil and gains innumerable blessings.

How many religious orders, the Oratorians, the Jesuits, the Theatines, the Barnabites, the Somaschites, the reformed orders, have encouraged the use of daily Communion for their priests, with the knowledge and approbation of St. Pius V., Clement VIII., and many other Popes and Bishops.

St. Ammon the Priest, whilst in the act of saying Mass, saw an angel on the right hand of the altar, who marked the brothers as they approached to receive the Blessed Sacrament and wrote their names in the Book of Life; those who abstained from Holy Communion he blotted out; and three days later they died.

Blosius relates that a soul appeared in the midst of great flames, and said she was severely tormented merely for having been remiss in going to Holy Communion; and added that she would be instantly set free if any one were to communicate devoutly for her intention.

The Communion was offered and the soul appeared once more, but brilliant as the sun, and ascended to Heaven.

The Ven. Mgr. Cacciaguerra concludes his treatise on Communion : "Now that I have said what I could on Holy Communion, and exhorted all to frequent the Sacrament according to the advice of the holy doctors and the general practice of the first age of the Church, I will add some facts and mention some wonderful effects which I have witnessed in several persons of my acquaintance. I have known men and women, previously abandoned to impurity, within a few weeks converted by frequent Communion to chaste and holy lives. I have known several conceive such a horror of this sin, that they would have suffered themselves to be cut into a thousand pieces rather than relapse into their carnal sins. And I have known public sinners, converted by the Blessed Sacrament ; some married, some led single lives and devoted themselves to works of piety, some became religious and attained great fervour of spirit. And still you hear it objected, that we no longer witness miracles, as in the lifetime of Jesus Christ ! And is it not a miracle, that abandoned sinners are converted to a holy life and serve God with all their hearts ?"

I might furnish a long list of similar cases of persons sanctified by the frequent use of Holy Communion. But what has been said, beloved souls, will arm you against the suggestions of the devil, and of wicked Christians in the world who condemn frequent Communion.

§ IV.

ON THE STATE OF FREQUENT COMMUNICANTS, AND ON THE SPIRITUAL DIRECTOR.

You must pray God to direct your spiritual Father to allow you Holy Communion according to your dispositions: for excess and insufficiency of food are both equally hurtful. The Good Shepherd provides food for His sheep, such as they can digest; the skilful Physician regulates the diet and the medicines according to the necessities of the patient; the wise Teacher shapes His instructions according to the capacity of His scholars. The Holy Ghost says in the Book of Proverbs; "*Thou hast found honey, eat what is sufficient for*

C

thee."* " *When thou shalt sit to eat with a prince, consider diligently what is set before thy face."* † St. Paul adds : " *Let a man prove himself, and so let him eat of that bread."* ‡ St. Thomas says the Blessed Eucharist is life to the good, but death to the wicked : how different are the effects of the same food ! St. Francis of Sales remarks, that it would be madness to recommend frequent Communion indiscriminately to every one. And the Ven. Patriarch Triepolo maintains that those only should communicate daily who have overcome the greater part of their evil inclinations. Lastly, the Ven. Franciotti lays down the principle, it is better not to attempt a good work, than to do it ill.

Pray God for a spiritual Father who is in favour of frequent Communion, who values Christian perfection, and wishes to see you make progress; pray that he may have knowledge, piety, and wisdom; pray that he may be superior to all human respect, to all temporal interests; pray that he may be a lover of prayer, silence, and retirement; pray that

* Proverbs xxv. 16. † Proverbs xxiii. 1.
‡ 1 Cor. xi. 28.

he may be stern and severe, rather than too easy with you. If God has given you such a guide, praise His Divine Majesty, and do not think of making any change.

If he scolds and blames and reprimands you for every little fault, if he checks your idle conversation, and forbids you to pay useless visits, you must not leave him for another. Fly to God, have recourse to Him; He will help you most, when help from man is denied you.

Pursue your course with simplicity, with humility, with the confiding reliance of a child; and beware of changing church or confessor for every breath of curiosity, or temptation, or mistrust.

Reverence your confessor as you would an angel, as holding the place of God. Speak to him always without concealment, with all frankness and sincerity. Let your conversation in the confessional be spiritual, devout, and holy.

Cherish a continual desire of Holy Communion. Make frequent use of spiritual communion, do so at least every hour. And do not be discouraged by the temptations or difficulties you meet with.

§ V.

COMFORT FOR TIMID AND PUSILLANIMOUS SOULS.

The devil commonly seeks to alarm persons who go frequently to Holy Communion, on the ground that their confessions have been sacrilegious, or that they have sinned where there is no sin, or that every action they perform is sinful, or that their life is full of faults; and, therefore, I may be allowed to address some words of comfort to timid and pusillanimous souls.

Do you wish to know, beloved souls, why the devil assails you with these fears? The reason is because he is envious of the great favours you receive from God. In fact when he saw Adam and Eve so highly favoured by God in the earthly paradise, his envy urged him to tempt them and deprive them of grace. The devil has the same object in exciting your fears; he wants to rob you of the grace of frequently receiving the Source of all good; and where he cannot accomplish this much, he hopes that you will be so much afflicted and troubled as to be unable to enjoy the Divine sweetness of the Blessed Sacrament. Always rejoice in the Lord. St. Antony, St. Francis, and St. Philip wished to see their children glad; for God is present where there is spiritual gladness, and the devil rules where there is melancholy.

Besides, the devil counts on robbing you of some of your merit, by inducing you not to trust your director as you ought, or by leading you to think that you and your confessor are losing precious time, or that you annoy your confessor, or that you weary him by repeating the same tale so often. The spider makes its web in cloudy weather, and the devil spreads his toils, when you give way to melancholy. Therefore, once more, always rejoice in the Lord.

Moreover, the devil adopts this course, because these scruples, this sadness, and gloom in reality displease God and wound Divine charity, inasmuch as the soul loses the love she ought to feel for God and even treats with God as if He were exacting. Oh, dear souls, did you only know how dear to God is your salvation, and what great favours He grants you every day! you would certainly not yield to scruples,

or sadness, or inordinate grief. Oh, if you would
understand the great jewel, the rich pledge
you possess in your souls, viz., the firm purpose
you entertain of suffering any evil rather than
offend the Divine Majesty! Of a certainty,
you may infer that you are always rightly dis-
posed to receive Holy Communion, so long as
you persevere in this determination, and that
you are in the grace of God, and, therefore,
can have no reason to give way to inordinate
sadness. For the love of God, banish all
melancholy from your heart and rejoice in
Jesus Christ.

Our Lord blessed St. Catharine of Bologna,
who had persevered in frequent Communion,
notwithstanding the dryness of soul and temptations against faith with which she was for a long
time tried, and said to her: "Those, who thus
resist the devil and frequently hear Mass, merit
more than they would have done, if they had
communicated with abundance of tears and
consolations."

The wonder, O beloved souls, and what
ought to amaze us, is that worldly persons, in
their blindness, keep aloof from God, in Whom
they might find salvation, glory, and every good.

thing. Their conduct pleases the devil, who knows how much he loses with those who frequent this Divine Sacrament. O ye blind worldlings, when will you open your eyes to see this great blessing?

Do you cherish these four truths in your hearts? (1) You stand in great need of this Sacrament. (2) Jesus invites you to the Eucharistic banquet, and threatens you with punishment if you refuse the nourishment of His sinless Body. (3) The saints all longed for this food. (4) This Adorable Sacrament brings with it all blessings.

§ VI.

THE REASON WHY ALL DO NOT RELISH HOLY COMMUNION.

There are four causes which hinder many from relishing the sweetness of the Blessed Sacrament.

Firstly, some do not receive in good dispositions.

Secondly, some are wanting in consideration.

Thirdly, some keep no guard on their hearts or senses.

Fourthly, some make little account of deliberate venial sins, of deliberate slight faults. Do you, however, guard against these as against a plague, and pray God that you may be in the disposition to die rather than yield to the least deliberate venial fault.

When you fall through human frailty, you must not lose courage or grow cold in your purpose of frequently receiving this great Gift. For, as St. Gregory says, God sometimes withholds the lesser grace from one to whom He has granted greater ones, and He allows those whom He has enabled to overcome grievous sins, to be overcome by lesser faults, as, for instance, immoderate laughter or mirth, a great readiness to take offence, and other similar faults, and this, that they may find occasion to give glory to God, through Whose grace they have vanquished more dreadful tyrants of their souls, and humble themselves, seeing they cannot by their own strength extirpate these smaller faults.

Taulerus will have it that God sometimes permits the existence of certain faults, such as anger, testiness, sharp words, &c., in His choice servants, in order to preserve them in great humility. These faults, like ashes, cover up the flames of Divine love; if you labour under such, be not alarmed, do not despond, but humble yourself much, and your faults will be an occasion of gaining great grace and abundant gifts from God.

Some persons, dearly beloved souls, when they fall into any fault, yield to grief and sorrow so much that they injure themselves more by their distress than they do by the fault which distresses them. And some, because sin naturally causes remorse, so far encourage remorse that their hearts are filled with bitterness, so that they fall into a state of continual disquiet, they never taste heavenly consolations, and they lose the courage and strength they formerly felt in trying to lead holy lives. And so when they commit a fault they seem to lose heart and the desire to do good.

Beloved, suffer not the devil to deceive you, but resist him and resist yourselves with great faith, and place all your reliance on God. And for your instruction know that this despondency may proceed from two causes. Firstly, it may proceed from a certain secret pride, which leads you unconsciously to think that you are somebody, and therefore ought never to fall into sin. An humble heart will cherish very different dispositions; it is conscious of its frailty, and will not be surprised when it is betrayed into many mistakes and errors. Hence St. Philip Neri was wont to say, "My Jesus, if Thou dost not help me I shall fall." Secondly, this despondency may spring from timorousness, the soul not understanding the grace of Redemption, and not knowing how to make use of the remedy which Christ has left us in His Passion and Death, for the cure of this want of courage.

§ VII.

MOTIVES WHY WE OUGHT TO FEEL CONFIDENCE IN FREQUENTING HOLY COMMUNION.

Consider the goodness of our Lord and never lose hope in His mercy, for He has fully satisfied for all your sins and the sins of all the world. How can you yield to any mistrust whilst under the protection of so great a Benefactor? What penance can you perform, what satisfaction can you offer to God comparable to that which His Son offered for you, from which all your penance and satisfaction derives its value and efficacy? And what are all the sins of the world in the presence of His merits but as a straw cast into a raging fire? Think that God addresses you in these words—*So long a time have I been with you, and have you not known me?** As if He would have said, "How long have you known Me in the Blessed Sacrament? Having found Me gentle, gracious, good, do you think me stern and severe? Do you not see that you offer a grievous insult to My great love?"

Does not the priest say to you, "Behold the Lamb of God, behold Him who takes away the sins of the world!" He does not call Him the the lion, but the Lamb, full of gentleness, armed only with kindliness, love, and mercy, not with sternness and severity.

He comes to give you life, not death; to fill your soul with peace, not with sadness; with the roses of devout thoughts, not with the thorns of anxious scruples.

Therefore rejoice. "Gladness of spirit," says St. Bonaventure, "is a sign of the grace of the Holy Ghost abiding in the soul."

Father Diego Stella says, "Banish from your

* St. John xiv. 9,

heart all mistrust and timorousness, for you can take no more dangerous foe with you into the battle, that is, into the way of perfection. Some persons fall into sadness because they do not serve God as they ought. Could such persons only see how much greater injury is caused them by their melancholy than by their sins, about which they are sad and dejected, they would gladly serve God with joy and zeal, humbling themselves on account of their weakness, and relying on the power of God."

This servant of God on one occasion was very much cast down on account of his failings, when he heard a voice, " Why art thou so unhappy? Come and cast all thy troubles into My side." This thought quite consoled him.

The Blessed Bartholomew de Martyribus used to say, " However imperfect you may be, God could easily make you a perfect man, if it were expedient for your salvation. And if it be His will that you should be tried in this way up to the time of your death, and even then experience irregular movements of anger, lust, and sadness, you must not lose courage."

A servant of God was wont to say that he was not afraid of the faults which he knew and detested, but of those faults which were hidden from him, or which he excused.

Another, that he was never surprised when he fell into faults, because he knew his weakness and wickedness; but he was surprised when he did not fall into them.

And a third, that falling into faults verified what St. Luke the Evangelist wrote in another sense;* it enables us to gather grapes from brambles, that is to say, the knowledge of the Divine goodness from our failings, and the figs of Divine consolation from the thorns of imperfections. And he added, that our Lord permits us to fall, that we may be urged to have recourse to Him.

St. Catharine of Siena says, that as a person who wishes to speak to a lord and have the pleasure of his conversation, does not remain in the ante-chamber, but seeks for admission into the audience-chamber, so we ought not to tarry in the ante-chamber of the consideration of our sins, but advance to the audience-chamber, that is, to the consideration of God's patient love and loving patience.

St. Augustine says that we ought to rejoice in

* St. Luke vi. 44.

D

the pain which arises from our sorrow for our sins, inasmuch as it implies the grace of God.

Venerable Bede says that St. Paul might have been lost if he had not had the sting of the flesh. Certainly many spiritual persons would be damned if God did not leave them subject to some faults.

St. Francis of Sales says, "Resist with energy the suggestions of the time of sadness, and though it seems your actions at such times are performed with coldness, persevere in them; for the enemy seeks to discourage your zeal for virtue by sadness, and when he sees you neglect none of your duties he will forbear to annoy you.

Thomas à Kempis says, "God daily gives two instructions to his elect; one to show them their own defects, the other to show them the goodness of God, Who bears with them so patiently.

Father Avila says, "O loving God, O God all love, how greatly he insults Thee who refuses to trust in Thee with all his heart!

St. Gertrude says, "As the bird does not always remain on her nest, but leaves it at times and soars aloft, and pours forth her song, and then returns to repose in her nest; so we should not always remain in the consideration of ourselves, we should rise to the contemplation of God's goodness and mercy, and from time to time turn our thoughts to the knowledge of ourselves."

I have treated this point at some length. I know how important it is you should understand it thoroughly.

§ VIII.

HOW THE DEVIL STRIVES TO PREVENT FREQUENT COMMUNION.

One of the great objects of the devil is to prevent the frequent reception of the Sacrament of the Altar; for he knows that nothing so upsets his power and baffles his designs as this Sacrament. For in this Sacrament the soul receives not only the grace of the Sacrament, the smallest degree of which is mightier than all the devils in Hell, but also the Author and Source of all grace. Moreover, the communicant makes acts of those virtues which are particularly distasteful to the devil, viz., Faith, Hope, Charity, Humility, Prayer, Contempt of the world, a resolution to fly from sin and all occasions of sin, and not only from mortal sins, but also from venial, as far as human frailty will allow. No wonder then if the devil try by every means to discourage frequent Communion.

1. If the devil whispers to you, " You are not worthy to receive ; Communion requires special preparation ; St. Paul tells you, ' Let a man prove himself before he eat, and he who eats unworthily eats damnation to himself. Answer him, " And who can be worthy ? If the sins of a week render me unworthy, those of a month or a year will render me much more so. The Council of Trent teaches me that it is only mortal sin that can make me unworthy, and that contrition with confession is the wedding garment, in which I may fearlessly approach the Sacrament. So, too, teach the Catechism, St. Thomas, St. Hilary, and the holy Fathers.

2. What will people say ? They will say you now mean to play the hypocrite.

Answer with St. Philip, " Better be an outcast in the service of God than in the service of the demon. None but mad persons are prevented from leaving their houses by the barking of small curs. The opinions of foolish men deserve no attention. We have no reason to blush for a good action, but only for those that are bad. When the world turns against us, we have a proof that we are pleasing to God."

3. Those who communicate frequently are bound to renounce all amusement, and commit themselves to a very rigorous and gloomy way of life. Answer.—True joy is found in the service of God, and words cannot tell the joy experienced by holy souls.

4. You are cold, dry, and insensible, How can you think of approaching this august Sacrament? Answer him : " Because I feel cold, I must draw near to the fire, and the sorer my infirmity, the greater my need of a remedy. How many have approached in a state of coldness, and gone away glowing."

5. The devil will exalt the great dignity of this Sacrament in your eyes to keep you aloof from it, under the pretext of humility, mixed up with pride, leading you to condemn those who communicate often. Ask him, Will the linen you constantly wear be cleaner if washed once a year or washed daily ?

6. Then he fills the imagination with thoughts

of impurity, of blasphemy, of infidelity, of
vanity, and in the night he occasions unclean
dreams. You must convince yourself that no
thought, however dreadful it be, is a sin, as long
as it is rejected by the will—nay, you merit in
the sight of God by banishing it.

7. He will tell you, you cannot help com-
mitting many sins, and you have many bad
habits. Ask in reply, What remedy so powerful
as this Sacrament? It is God's best gift to
beautify the soul and cleanse it from every
stain. Experience brings this truth home to us.
If you wish your soul to be beautiful, fail not
to partake of the Flesh of thy Heavenly Spouse
every day.

8. Lastly, he will tell you that too much
familiarity with God is unseemly, that it leads to
contempt or to communicating by routine. He
will ask you, Are not many who communicate
frequently passionate, selfish, in fact, full of
defects, like other men? Are not many priests
who celebrate Mass every day only more
hardened by doing so? Mind your needle-
work, you pious woman, that is your occupa-
tion. Answer him, Those who shun familiarity
with God are too familiar with the devil.

Familiarity with creatures breeds contempt, but not familiarity with God, Who is perfection itself. At least frequent Communion will be a holy routine, a virtuous habit. Who is without defect or failing? Every one can see the evil; allowance is not made for the good. The passions in us may be restrained, they cannot be quite uprooted. Look at the priests of holy and exemplary life. No one can communicate devoutly and fail to make progress. In a fertile garden pluck the flowers and fruit, and do not look after thorns. Must we abstain from wine, because there are so many sour grapes? Must we lay aside knives, because there are so many murders? Let the devil say his say; you do the best you can for yourself.

When men who cannot appreciate this Treasure strive to cool your ardour by foolish reasonings, refer them to many great Doctors ot the Church who have written in defence of frequent Communion, Fulvia Androzi, to Loarte, to Cacciaguerra, to Emundo Auger, to Salmeron, to Labata, to Pietri di S. Bonaventura, to Cristofero Morerro, to Giacomo Baro, to Varonio, to Giovanni Sanzio, to P. D. Paolo Barisoni, to the venerable Patriarch of Venice, Gio. Tiepolo, in the tenth book and the second part of his " Considerazioni del B Sacramento."

And you, my beloved daughters, who are so tenderly devoted to the Blessed Sacrament, you must preserve your souls free from every breath of mortal sin, and as far as you can from venial sin too, and if you wish to prepare yourselves to receive this great gift worthily every day, banish from your minds all vain and worldly ideas, all thoughts of honours, pleasures, and amusements, all concessions to the senses or self-love, and endeavour to adorn yourselves with the holy virtues of purity, humility, patience, charity, meekness, piety, and the like. Do not set your heart on receiving consolation or sensible devotion in daily Communion ; do not covet raptures, visions, revelations, and other spiritual favours, but aim at the acquisition of true and solid virtues, by imitating the life of your Heavenly Spouse, Jesus Christ, and of Mary, His Blessed Mother.

§ IX.

CONSIDERATIONS FITTED TO EXCITE DEVOTION IN HOLY COMMUNION.

If my heart is the temple of God, the tabernacle of the Blessed Trinity, the sanctuary of the Holy Ghost, ought I not to preserve it in all possible cleanness, purity, and brightness? Ought I not to banish far from me all wicked thoughts, all unholy desires?

If each time that I receive Holy Communion I become in a manner like the Mother of God, ought I not to desire and ask for all those virtues which the Mother of God possessed? Ought I not to say with perfect resignation, "Behold the handmaid of the Lord, may it be done to me according to Thy word."

If in Holy Communion my body is touched by God, ought I not to preserve it, support it, and cherish it for God alone? Ought I not to look upon it as a relic, as a thing consecrated to God? Can I ever permit myself or others to lay hands upon it without reverence? Must I not guard it to keep it in purity?

The sepulchre in which Christ was laid was new, and had been used for no one, the winding-sheet in which the body was wrapped was white : the corporal must be spotless, and the host without flaw. Ought not my soul to be pure and spotless ?

Where God is, there is Paradise. In Paradise the will of God is perfectly carried out, His glory alone is sought. Ought I not then seek in all things the honour and glory of my God, and place myself in conformity with his blessed will? Thy will be done on earth as it is in Heaven.

How gladly Martha entertained our Blessed Lord ! Shall not I receive Him with joy ? Shall not I forget my unworthiness, to think of the goodness and liberality of my Lord, Who deigns to take up His abode with me, Who stoops to enrich my poverty, to supply for my shortcomings, and to endow me with endless blessings ?

Whenever I communicate, my Spouse Jesus rests upon my tongue. Ought I not to watch over it, to curb it, to employ it in the praise of my Saviour, in speaking of Him, in making Him known ?

He gives us His Blood. Shall not I give blood for blood, and long to shed my blood for so dear and loving a Lord ?

Were some prince or king or emperor to invite me as a guest to his table, I should never appear with the slightest spot upon my face, or the least stain upon my dress. I should strive to present myself adorned to the best of my power. How I should think myself favoured and honoured! What should be my conduct towards the mighty Monarch of Heaven and earth?

He gives Himself to me in the Blessed Sacrament with infinite love. Why should I not, if it were possible, receive Him with infinite love, and repay love for love?

Every day He grants new favours, new lights, new graces, new consolations, new blessings, and merits. Ought I not ever love Him, ever serve, praise, and glorify Him, and desire that all men may seek Him and love Him and praise Him and glorify Him?

Jesus gives Himself wholly to me, with all that He is, His Divinity, His attributes, His Humanity, His Soul, His Body, His Blood. Shall I not give myself wholly to Him? Thine am I, save me. I desire nothing, I ask for nothing beyond Thee, my Jesus, beloved Heart of my heart.

William of Paris says four things should be
considered in the Blessed Sacrament : (1) The
miracle of God's power, by which the bread
and wine we see are so wonderfully changed
into the Body and Blood of Christ which we do
not see, and the appearances of bread and
wine are preserved, though the substances are
no longer present. (2) The wisdom and pro-
vidence of God, Who has provided in this
useful and most suitable manner for the nourishment of our souls, so that the very outward
form of this food, the form of bread, invites
us to partake of it.   (3) The riches of the
goodness of God, Who so readily spreads this
banquet for us, and does so with so much joy
and gladness. (4) The memorial of God's
mercy, Who did not spare His only Son, but
gave Him up to die, that we might possess
Him for ever even in this world.   The thought
should fill us with wonder and amazement.

St. Mechtildis considered four things in this
august Sacrament : (1) The love of God, Who
had thought of her from all eternity ; (2) Who
created her, knowing how ungrateful she would
prove herself to His Divine Majesty ; (3) Who
died for her on the Cross, and satisfied the

Eternal Father for her sins by His Precious
Blood; (4) Who chose to abide in this Sacra-
ment from love for her, to feed her with His
Flesh and cleanse her soul in His Blood.

§ X.

OTHER CONSIDERATIONS TO EXCITE US TO
DEVOTION IN HOLY COMMUNION.

1. What would be the language of a person
visited now by some Prince, now by a King, now
by an Emperor, now by a Bishop, a Cardinal, or
the Pope? What if visited to day by an angel,
and on the next day by another? What will you
say whom God Almighty visits? Are you not
lost in amazement? Do you not exult with joy?
Do you not cry with St. Elizabeth: "Whence
is this to me, that the Mother of my Lord should
come to me;" or with the Blessed Virgin: "My
soul doth magnify the Lord, and my spirit doth
rejoice in God my Saviour.

2. If the Queen of Saba was delighted and
astonished at the splendid order observed in the
Court of Solomon, ought not you to feel gladness and amazement at the visit of Christ to your
soul? If the Magi were so filled with joy on

E

beholding the star which directed them to the manger, ought not you to rejoice, when visited by God and by all Paradise? Is it possible that you can be buried in sadness and affliction at the time of Holy Communion?

3. Were a subject to receive frequent gifts from his Prince, he would value them highly, and still more would he value them if the Prince in person were to present these gifts. And if God were to send you some precious object by the hands of an angel, you would certainly prize it. Yet God, the Lord of Lords, the King of Kings descends to you to honour you with His Divine presence and He offers you the treasure of treasures, Himself, His Flesh and His Blood, and all the gifts purchased by that Blood, His Soul and His Divinity. Are we not lost in amazement? Ought we not to keep a perpetual holiday to celebrate this wonder? Ought we not to thank His Divine Majesty day and night for this goodness? The heart that receives such a favour should surely overflow with joy!

4. If Daniel was so astonished when God sent him food in the lion's den by the hands of Habacuc, what should be the astonishment of those who are fed with the Body of Christ and

honoured by His Divine presence, beset as they are by demons, eager to devour them?

5. If Solomon rejoiced so greatly when he beheld the Temple completed, the soul should rejoice in Holy Communion, for she has become the temple of God. If we could only see the angels gathering round each communicant! if we could hear their song, Holy, Holy, Holy! Certainly, my beloved daughters, sadness and melancholy would vanish from our hearts, gladness, joy and peace would take possession of our souls.

6. You have become the tabernacle of the Most Holy Trinity. For when you receive Jesus Christ, you receive by *concomitance* God the Father and God the Holy Ghost. In consequence, your soul has become a most glorious heaven, in which the high and living God dwells. Is not this something?

7. As often as you communicate you are placed on a level with the Mother of God, you become the Spouse of Jesus, the daughter of the Virgin Mary, and like Simeon you are privileged to embrace Jesus Christ. What a favour! What a privilege! what a blessing! And men esteem it so lightly! they think of it so seldom! O God, where is faith?

8. You become the precious reliquary of Jesus Christ. You would be delighted if you were presented with a costly reliquary filled with highly prized relics : you would be at a loss to express your gratitude. What will you say, now that you are become the reliquary of the Humanity and Blood of Jesus Christ? Your heart should be inundated with joy and gladness.

9. Had you lived at the time when Christ was buried, you would have esteemed yourself fortunate had you been allowed to bury Him in your own garden. The owner of the garden which contained the sepulchre of Christ need envy no one. Yet is not yours a greater privilege, to receive Christ living into your body and soul? Is it not a higher privilege to be, as it were, the tomb of Christ living, than to be the owner of the tomb in which He lay dead some forty hours? And if the latter be held in such honour, how much is due to the former? Oh think on the magnificent gift you daily receive and be thankful.

10. Had you lived with Christ, would you not have thought it a great privilege to be allowed to kiss His hand, or to touch even His dress every day? What say you now? with your

perishable body you may touch the Flesh and Body of Jesus your glorious impassible and immortal Lord.

11. Had Jesus during His life on earth even once deigned to take up His abode in your house, would you not have rejoiced and accounted yourself highly favoured? And is it not a higher favour to receive Him in His glory, His beauty and His immortality?

12. You are constituted a Paradise. For where God is found, there is Paradise. When you are tired, imagine you hear Jesus Christ say to you: "This day thou shalt be with Me in Paradise." Rest satisfied and rejoice.

13. Had Jesus during His lifetime only once even invited you to sit at table with Him, you would have thought yourself happy and favoured. What say you now? He feeds you frequently with His own Body and Blood. Did any King, any mother ever act thus?

14. In Holy Communion you receive the greatest favours, honours, distinctions, and marks of kindness which a creature can receive in this world. For with the Body and Blood of Christ you partake of all the merits and advantages which He purchased for you, and you can say:

" He hath not dealt so with any nation." How many Kings and Princes are there who receive not such favours and kindness from God ?

15. When you communicate, imagine that you apply your mouth to the side of Jesus Christ. This is the advice of St. John Chrysostom. St. Catharine of Siena and St. Frances of Rome followed this practice. Approach and partake of the merits, the virtues, the graces, the spirit of Christ Himself. The Eternal Father will look upon you with the same paternal loving look which He casts upon His own Son. Can any privilege surpass this? Can there be condescension more gentle? " Look on me."

16. When a Prince bestows a trifling object on a poor person, the gift is greatly prized. What say you, if the giver be infinite, if the gift be infinite, if it be given with infinite love? God is the Giver. God is the Gift. You receive it from God and through God. God invites you to receive it. God Himself waits on us at this banquet. Can more be said? What an exchange, exclaims St. Teresa, we may give our love for the love of God !

17. Whilst the Jews were making ready the gall, the thorns, the nails for Christ ; whilst they were

preparing sufferings and pains for Him, His thoughts were fixed on providing for us nourishment, honours, consolations, joys, favours, and incredible delights, the choicest gifts of Heaven.

18. How many are ignorant of all these truths! How many have the knowledge and yet have no desire to frequent Holy Communion! How many have the desire and yet have it not in their power to communicate? How many have it in their power and are without priests? How many souls in Germany, in Scotland, in France, in England, in Poland and other countries would be thankful for the crumbs which fall from our table? How many would think themselves happy if they could communicate once every month? How many religious are there who do not enjoy this privilege at God's hand?

Say, then, what return shall I make to God for this signal privilege? This day I will take the chalice, how bitter soever it may be, which He may send me. I will bless His name, and it shall be my consolation. I will pay my vows to Him. I will renounce all vanity. I will die to myself and to all the world, for " Precious in the sight of the Lord is the death of His Saints."

O Jesus, my love, grant that I may joyfully drink the golden chalice of love and suffering as You have done for me.

§ XI.

SOME SPIRITUAL COUNSELS.

I exhort you, O favoured souls, to imagine that your angel guardian addresses you now with one, now with another of these words : " *Whom didst thou receive this morning ? Whom shalt thou receive to-morrow ?* " *Mind thyself. What is it to Thee ? Do thou follow Me. Glory to God on high. Lift up your hearts. Hosanna in the highest. My heart, where art thou ? Whither art thou going ? What are thy thoughts ? What are thy actions ? God beholds thee. Remember eternity. A pure intention. Attention. Deep, strong and generous devotion.*

Conclude your actions by saying : " But do Thou, O Lord, have mercy on us. Thanks be to God." In these words you ask pardon for your defects and you thank God for what you have done well. Sing with St. Cecily : *Preserve my heart and my body from all stain, that I may not be confounded—Fiat cor meum et corpus meum immaculatum, ut non confundar.*

Some persons think themselves holy and perfect because they communicate daily: and they live without any internal or external recollection. They are mostly restless, sensitive, impatient, weak minded, obstinate, careless in the management of their homes: in their charges and offices they cannot brook the least word, or pass over the slightest negligence; their tongues are unbridled, their manners are unrestrained, their consciences are dull, they have no care for real perfection, they are utterly unmortified; and they are bent on living after their own whims.

My beloved daughters, be not like these persons. Do you join to daily Communion great care to shun all vices, sins, and defects, however small they may be: all pride, vainglory, impatience, loquaciousness, impurity. Join to the exercise of all virtues, a careful watch over your heart, humility, patience, purity, obedience, prayer, recollection, charity. Place all your delight in God, think of Him, speak of Him. Under all circumstances, submit to His blessed will; desire to be united with Him, and for this end set at nought the railings of men, and self-will, with a view to self-contempt and the breaking of your self-will, your disordered appetites and attachments.

Further I exhort you to put a check on your words in times of trial. Let no words escape your lips at such times but: May the Name of the Lord be for ever blessed. Thy will be done. Blessed be God. O good Jesus. My Jesus. My beloved Jesus. Jesus, Mary, &c., &c.

You will be truly happy if you are faithful in the few things God may appoint for you from day to day, and receive all things as coming from His well loved hands and refer all things to Him. He says: "He who would come after Me, let him deny his own will, take up his cross daily and follow Me." Elsewhere He says too: "Well done, thou good and faithful servant, because thou hast been faithful over few things, I will place thee over many things. Enter into the joy of thy Lord."

Pursue your course between hope and fear and keep in your company the two sisters, humility and obedience. If you preserve these dispositions by all means communicate every day; let the world talk as it pleases, you do your good work in right earnest. "Hold fast that which is good." In place of a hundred thousand reasons you have the august words of your Heavenly Spouse Jesus Christ. "He who eats My flesh and drinks My blood, shall possess eternal life. He shall remain in Me, and I in him."

Persevere pure, joyful, constant, contented, faithful till death to your beloved Spouse Jesus Christ. Filled with raptures of joy often sing to Him : Long live the pure love of Jesus Christ in the Blessed Sacrament, my only treasure, my only possession. May it live for ever !

ROEHAMPTON :
PRINTED BY JAMES STANLEY.

www.ingramcontent.com/pod-product-compliance
Lightning Source LLC
Chambersburg PA
CBHW022042080426
42733CB00007B/950